Junior Science
bouncing and rolling

Terry Jennings

Illustrations by David Anstey

Gloucester Press
New York · London · Toronto · Sydney

About this book

You can learn all about bouncing and rolling in this book. There are many different experiments for you to try. You will find out why some objects bounce and roll and others don't, why some balls bounce higher than others, how to measure balls, how hard a rolling ball can push and much more.

First Paperback Edition 1990
ISBN 0 531 17500 6

First published in the
United States in 1988 by
Gloucester Press
387 Park Avenue South
New York, NY 10016

ISBN 0 531 17085 3

Library of Congress Catalog
Card Number: 87-82971

© BLA Publishing Limited 1988

This book was designed and produced by BLA
Publishing Limited, TR House, Christopher
Road, East Grinstead, Sussex, England

A member of the Ling Kee Group
London Hong Kong Taipei Singapore New York
Printed in Great Britain

Look at the picture. It shows different kinds of balls. Some of the balls are soft and some are hard. Some are solid and some are hollow. And some are bouncy and some are not. Some balls fit into more than one of these groups.

When this rubber ball was dropped on the floor it bounced. But when the cotton ball was dropped on the floor it did not bounce. Of all the objects in the picture only the rubber ball is really bouncy.

Here are two balls of the same size. The green ball is made of rubber and the brown ball is made of wood. The green ball bounces very high. The brown ball hardly bounces at all. The balls bounce differently because they are made of different materials.

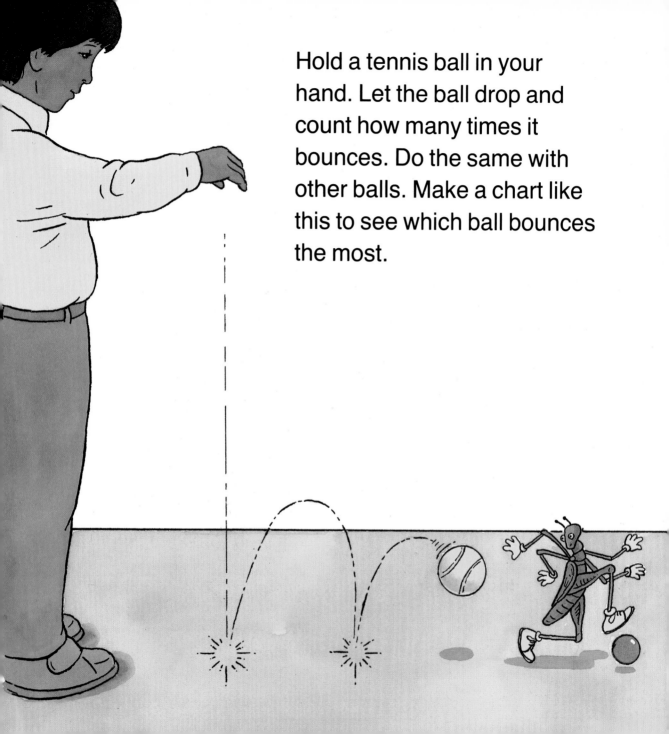

Hold a tennis ball in your hand. Let the ball drop and count how many times it bounces. Do the same with other balls. Make a chart like this to see which ball bounces the most.

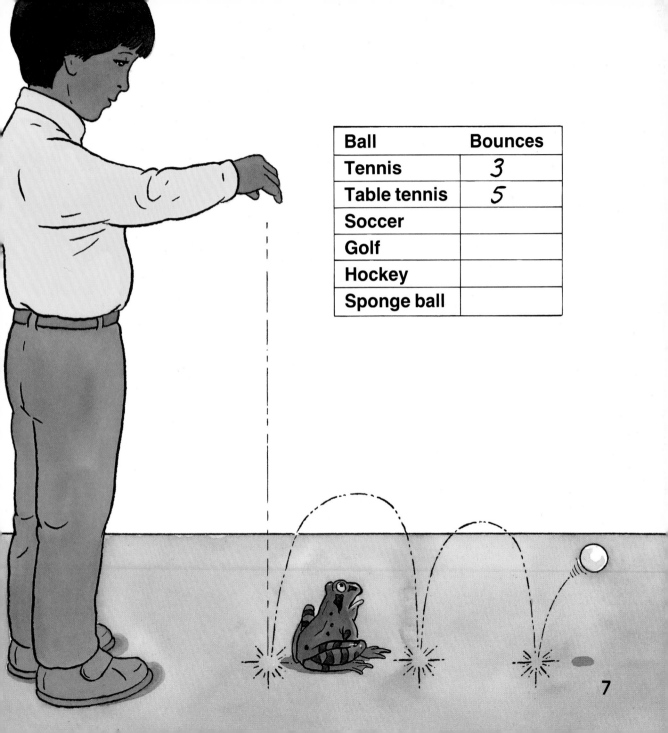

Ball	Bounces
Tennis	3
Table tennis	5
Soccer	
Golf	
Hockey	
Sponge ball	

7

You can measure how high the balls can bounce. Mark a strip of cardboard in inches and stick it to a table leg. Let one of the balls roll off the table. Mark on the card how high the ball bounces. Do this for each of the balls in turn. In the picture the table tennis ball and the sponge ball bounced the highest.

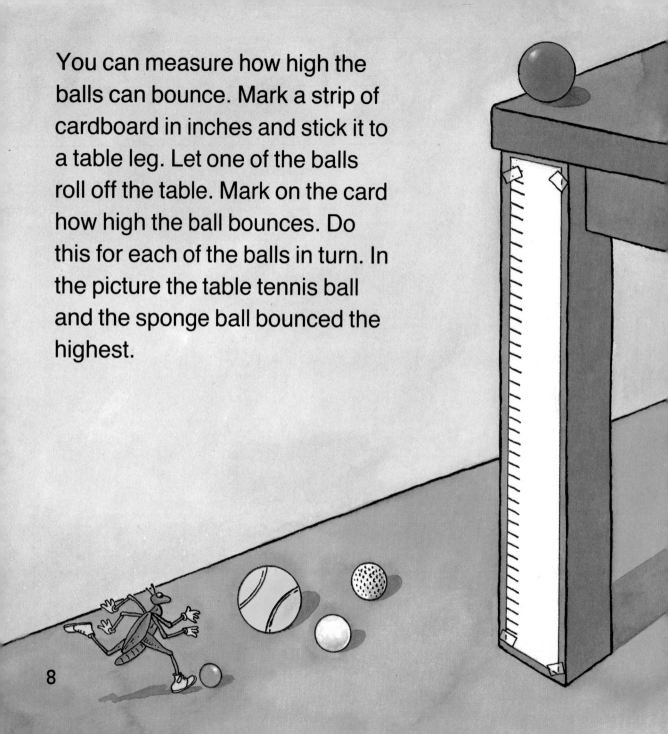

Some balls are good bouncers and some are poor bouncers. Some good bouncers are made of rubber. They can be solid or hollow. Other good bouncers are made of hollow plastic. The poor bouncers are made of solid wood, plastic, metal or glass.

marble

wooden ball

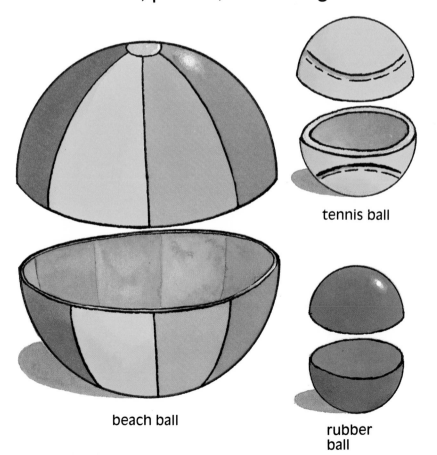

beach ball

tennis ball

rubber ball

snooker ball

9

If you blow a beach ball full of air the ball will become hard. It will then bounce very high. If you let a little air out of the ball it will not bounce as high. The air inside a full beach ball helps to make the ball very springy. Then the ball bounces well.

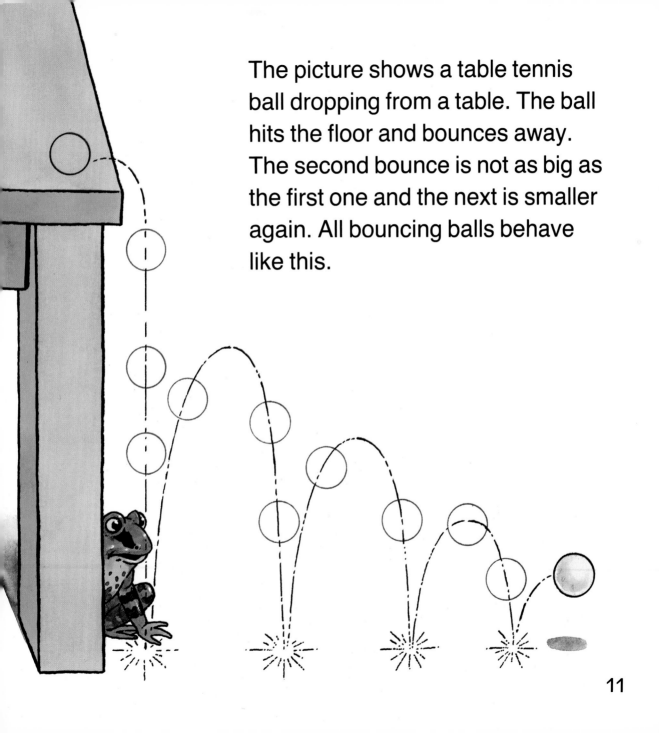

The picture shows a table tennis ball dropping from a table. The ball hits the floor and bounces away. The second bounce is not as big as the first one and the next is smaller again. All bouncing balls behave like this.

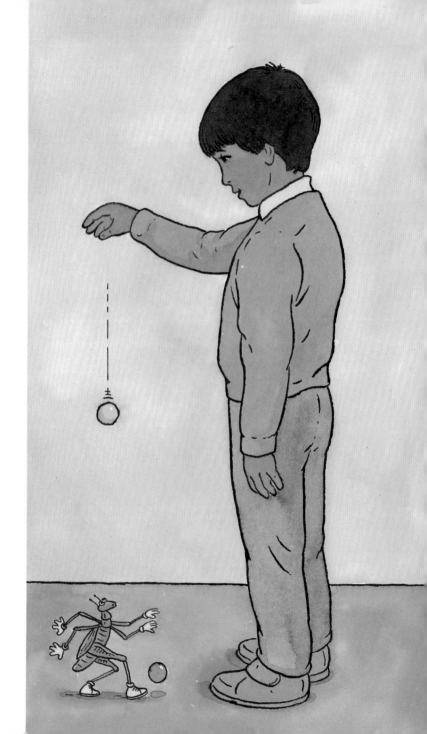

12

Take some modeling clay and roll it into two balls the same size. Drop one ball to the floor. Then stand on a chair and drop the other. This is a picture of how the balls will probably look.

The ball which has been dropped from the chair will hit the floor hardest. It will be dented the most.

Try bouncing some balls on different
surfaces. Drop a rubber ball onto a hard floor.
The ball will bounce high.

Drop the ball onto a thick rug and it will not bounce as high. If you drop the ball onto sand it will not bounce at all.

Now drop a ball made of modeling clay onto a hard floor. It will not bounce at all. But drop the ball on a thick rubber mat and it will bounce. This is because the mat is springy. The springy mat forces the ball upward.

You can measure balls. Put a ball between two big blocks. This will show how far it is across the ball. Now measure the gap between the two blocks. This measurement is called the diameter of the ball.

Some shapes roll better than others. Here only the ball and the cylinder will roll down this slope easily.

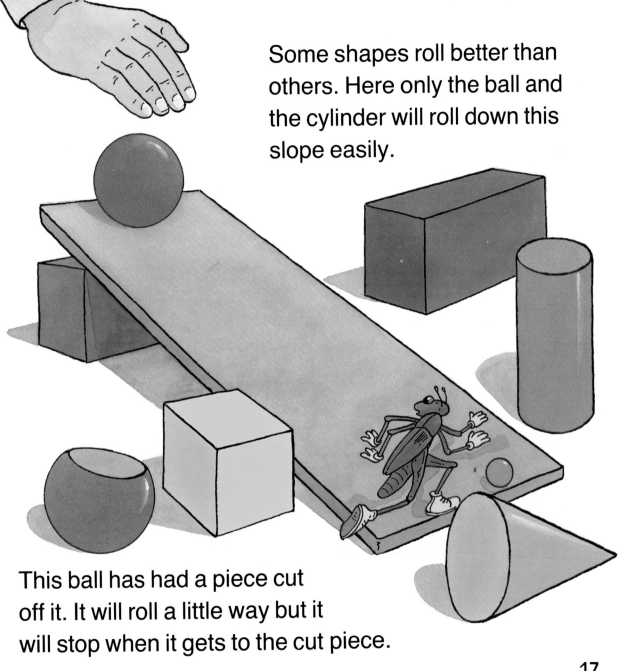

This ball has had a piece cut off it. It will roll a little way but it will stop when it gets to the cut piece.

Put a book under one end of a plank so that it makes a slope. Roll a ball down the slope and measure how far it goes. Put two books under the plank and you will see that the ball rolls further. This is because the slope is steeper.

If you try rolling the ball on rough carpet, the ball will not roll as far. The carpet soon stops the ball by rubbing on it.

19

You can measure how hard a rolling ball can push. Rest a cardboard tube on books like this. Near the bottom of the tube put a box. Mark where the edge of the box is. Put a marble in the tube.

The marble will bump into the box and move it. Measure how far the box has moved. Next put a golf ball into the tube. It will roll down and push the box. Again measure how far the box has moved. The golf ball will push the box further because it is heavier than the marble.

The red ball is rolling down the slope.
It is going to hit the other four balls. All
of the balls will move but the green
ball will move the most.

22

glossary

Here are the meanings of some words you may have used for the first time in this book.

bounce: to jump back when thrown against something hard or when dropped on something hard.

diameter: a line drawn from one side of a circle to the other passing through the center.

hollow: not solid, having an empty space inside.

plank: a long flat piece of wood.

slope: a line or surface which goes gradually upward or downward.

solid: not hollow, having no space inside.

tube: a hollow length of rubber, metal, plastic, cardboard or other material.

index